Contents

Introduction

There's a common misconception that success comes easy for some people and is very difficult for most others. Generally speaking, this is simply not true.

The truth is, success is not easy for anyone. There are hidden factors that separate successful people from non-successful people.

Of course, right place / right time, who you know, innate abilities, environment, and personal starting point *can* play a role in the path to success.

But, for the most part, success is derived from hard work, smart work, dedication, diligence, practice, motivation, and perseverance. And, at the core of all of these factors is what is known as self-discipline.

Self-discipline is the ability to manage one's thoughts and actions in a manner that leads towards an end goal, while bypassing obstacles, avoiding distractions, and resisting temptations that lead away from that end goal.

The art of self-discipline extends about as far back as human consciousness.

From the very beginnings of human development, self-discipline played a role in survival:

> He who stored enough food from foraging or hunting in order to have enough when the food supply was minimal or non-existent was the generally one who survived.

> He who built a sturdy home (regardless of material) that could withstand the elements of the natural world – be it weather, wildlife, or temperature – was generally the one who survived.

> He who put together enough clothing to withstand the temperature changes in the surrounding environment also was the one who generally survived.

Self-discipline comes in various forms.

In its most basic form, self-discipline is simply the practice of resisting any urge that doesn't relate to your current focus or goals. This form of self-discipline is called restraint.

Another form of self-discipline includes ignoring or refraining from acknowledging physical discomfort, distress, pain, and unease. This form of self-discipline is called self-control. Self-control also includes training your body to perform physical feats not normally a part of the human condition, such as walking on fire stones,

Self-discipline includes accepting the conditions that are temporary and waiting for the desired results without internal stress and strife. This form of self-discipline is called patience.

Self-discipline can also include not giving up on intentions or desired results when things become difficult, challenging, or frustrating. It's finishing what you started, even when the going gets tough. This form of self-discipline is dedication and perseverance.

And, self-discipline can include the sheer mental strength to keep moving ahead, even when obstacles seem insurmountable. This form of self-discipline is called will-power.

It doesn't matter what aspect of self-discipline you decide to work on first... they all go hand-in-hand. And, as you increase your self-discipline in one regard, the others will naturally increase (even if only slightly).

The first step, of course, is to resolve yourself to increase your self-discipline. If you're not ready to do so or if you simply don't want to, you'll find it very difficult to create a plan and to stick to it.

Remember: increasing your self-discipline is a choice, not a matter of circumstance. ANYONE can improve their self-discipline with a little dedication.

Instant Gratification vs. Delayed Gratification

While many think of self-discipline as containing discomfort, pain ("no pain, no gain"), or frustrating self-sacrifice, the true meaning does not necessarily have negative connotations attached to it.

Self-discipline is the art of rejecting instant gratification in place of delayed gratification and results

We are a society of immediate gratification enthusiasts. We want what we want, when we want it... and, we want it NOW.

This is compounded by the fact that we're constantly being bombarded with information and stimulating gratification through our mobile devices, social media accounts, and various corporate enterprises that reward us for taking immediate action.

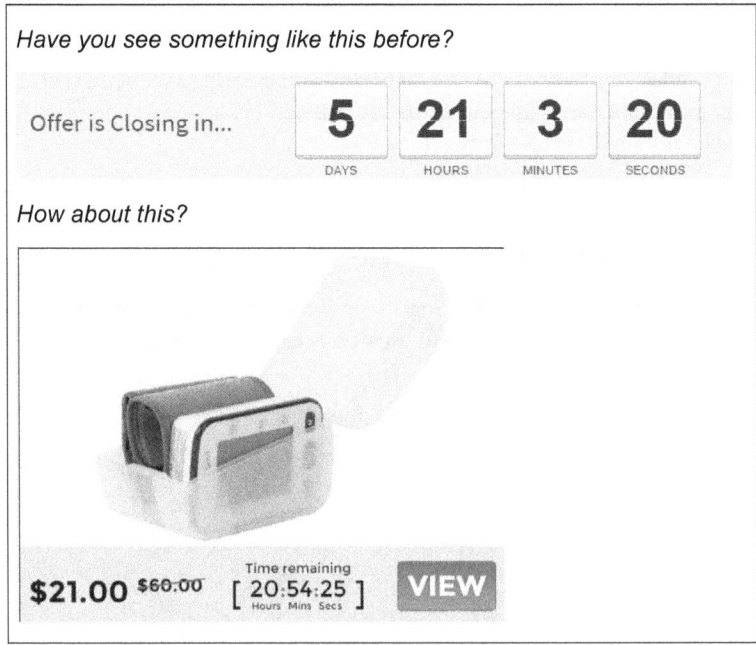

As a society at large, we're being conditioned to continue seeking out instant gratification, while self-discipline is going by the wayside.

Scientists have actually been studying the topic of delayed gratification versus instant gratification for decades. One of the most famous studies, called the *Stanford Marshmallow Experiment,* was conducted in 1972.

During the study, researchers placed a young child in a room with one marshmallow or cookie on a table. The child was then told that the researcher had to leave the room for a little while, and that if the marshmallow or cookie was still there when he returned, the child would get two marshmallows or two cookies.

As you can assume, most of the children ate the first marshmallow or cookie long before the researcher returned.

Impulse control isn't well-developed in children younger than the age of 7 – they also don't have much of an ability think and plan for the future. The nice, tasty marshmallow or cookie sitting in the middle of the table in front of them is all they really could see, and most of them went for it.

But, the researchers decided to go one step further with their study. They waited until the children were 18 years old, and then evaluated them on several factors, including educational achievement.

The results showed that the children who were able to successfully resist the temptation of the single marshmallow – and, instead waited for two in return – generally had significantly better results in school than the ones who quickly succumbed to temptation.

Along with that, the children who resisted the immediate temptation and sought delayed gratification were linked to have more positive personality characteristics like assertiveness, dependability, desire to learn, self-reliance, trustworthiness, as well as the ability to cope with frustration.

The children who sought the immediate gratification of, stubborn, had a tendency to be overwhelmed by stress, and were the marshmallow in front of them, however, generally were more impulsive, indecisive more prone to feel jealousy and envy.

Around 2011, this study was followed-up on some of the original test subjects.

The results showed that those who were better at delaying gratification as children continued to do so as adults.

In fact, the part of the brain known as the ventral striatum -- an area generally linked to addictions -- was shown to be more active in those that were unable to resist the temptation and immediate gratification.

Understanding the difference between instant gratification and delayed gratification, and allowing yourself to forgo short-term stimulation, instead focusing on long-term goals and aspirations is one of the first steps towards achieving better self-discipline.

If you really want to lose weight, you're going to have to recognize when you're tempted to eat a delicious cookie or fried goodie, resist the urge to do so, and focus on what your end goal – the delayed pleasure of being in a different weight class.

If you're looking to be able to complete a work project or school assignment within a period of time, you're going to have to recognize when you're tempted to go out and play a sport, flip on the TV or a video game, or go and sleep (unless you're completely exhausted), resist those urges, focus on the end result of a completed project, and forge ahead with accomplishment.

In the end, anything that provides *instant gratification* is likely only temporary… and, it likely won't benefit you in the future – which means that you'd have to continually expose yourself to it in order to derive future pleasure.

Instead, work on applying self-control and focus on what you really want in / out of life. The satisfaction of accomplishing a bigger goal, getting what you really want, and 'winning' in the sense that you're seeking can be far greater than any temporary high.

Understanding Yourself

A big factor in developing strong self-discipline is having an understanding of who you truly are and what you like / don't like, as well as what drives you, what tempts you, and what motivates you.

By understanding yourself, you'll get to learn your strengths and your weaknesses, which can help you focus on which areas need improvement – such as being able to resist the temptation of _____ (fill in your most notorious vice).

One of the most important pieces to understanding yourself is to know how much (or, how little) self-respect you have – and, then to increase it.

Having a strong sense of self-respect helps make it easier to resist short-term temptations of satisfaction (in order to make yourself feel better by external factors) and focus on your longer-termed goals and desires… since you already feel good about yourself, you don't need to compensate by feeding into needless vices and distractions that don't serve a purpose towards your goals.

When you lack self-respect, you're constantly seeking outside stimuli in order to feel better – you buy new toys, new cars, new devices; you watch endless TV, you feel compelled to fill your life with 'stuff' because you don't find any sort of satisfaction without it.

You're constantly looking to fill a void because your sense of self-worth is low – and, this can lead to compulsive actions, impulse buying, and saying things that you may not necessarily mean.

A lack of self-respect can also lead to lethargy, laziness, procrastination, and even depression.

This is why it's vital that you focus on improving your self-respect and sense of self-worth. It is at the core of achieving better self-discipline.

There are many ways to improve your sense of self-worth. But, the most effective methods do have to come from inside of you rather than from outside.

Positive reinforcement from friends or family members (or, even from yourself) can help. Giving yourself a 'job-well-done' sense of appreciation every time you accomplish something that was a challenge for you is important. And, hearing the appreciation and congratulations from loved ones is also a great way to *feel better* about yourself.

Accepting your failures as learning experiences and moving on is also very important for your self-respect. Many times, we can take our losses and failures to heart and 'beat ourselves up' for it – whether emotionally, psychologically, or even through physical punishment.

We can deny ourselves an aspect of life that we love as a way of trying to force ourselves into not failing again. However, in general, positive reinforcement can be much more effective than negative action / punishment.

It's okay if you fail sometimes. It's okay if you lose sometimes. It's nearly impossible to be perfect all of the time.

So, relax and accept that sometimes you won't come out on top. Use those times to learn from your mistakes, errors in judgment or action, or missteps, and grow from there.

Keep the faith in the outcome you desire is an indirect way of improving your self-respect. It can sometimes be hard to see and believe that we can achieve the outcome we're looking for. And, this is directly because we lack the confidence that we can achieve it.

Self-doubt can infect the mind… and, when it runs out of control, self-respect gets reduced dramatically.

Therefore, focusing your attention on the future desired outcome and not allowing yourself to be stressed or anxious about *not* reaching that outcome is a surefire way to improve your own self-respect.

And, *trusting yourself,* including your deepest desires, gut instinct, and feelings of what is right / wrong go a long way towards improving your self-worth. The unique thing about life (whether human, animal, reptile, insect, or plant) is that we pretty much all of have a deeply embedded survival instinct.

This survival instinct may or may not always work in our favor – but, for the most part, it is at the core of who we are… and, it allows us to know things such as whether or not we like a certain food, activity, or other human.

Generally speaking, when we really know and understand ourselves, our instincts can be pretty accurate. And, when you learn to trust yourself and your instincts, you start to gain more respect for yourself and more discipline in what you're looking to achieve / accomplish.

Self-Accountability

To truly gain an understanding of yourself, you'll need to accept responsibility for your decisions, your words, and your actions.

Coming to terms with the fact that the conditions of your life are in large part created by you – your choice of employment, your choice of who you surround yourself with, your choice of neighborhood, your choice of hobbies / activities, your choice of health standards – and, you have the control to change / modify them as you see fit.

Most of the world wanders through life thinking that life happens to them, that fate or destiny is uncontrollable, and that they have no say in their outcome(s).

The truth is, while bad things do happen sometimes, we're mostly in control of our life – and, we're certainly in control of our choices and how we interact with the world.

Grasping self-accountability is a key element to learning about yourself and increasing your self-discipline.

In short, the sooner you stop the excuses and let go of the idea that you're not in control of your own life, the sooner you'll find that your ability to develop your life, your freedom, and your success grows.

Write it all down.

As you learn about yourself, your goals, your desires, your weaknesses, and your strengths, take the time to write your thoughts down. This not only reinforces the ideas that you've developed, but also serves as a reminder to be reviewed any time you feel that you are slipping or falling out of self-discipline.

Writing down your goals and your intentions is also a great way to ingrain it into your mind. Seeing it visually can be more powerful than simply thinking it – it can provide an extra sense of motivation and stimulation by combining one of the senses (sight) with the brain activity of thought.

When you read it aloud and / or record it and replay it, you can also combine the sense of hearing, which further stimulates recollection and reinforcement.

And, writing down your goals can also help you organize the steps you need to take to get to those goals. Perhaps, your goal is to be able to run a marathon.

By writing it down, it may occur to you that you can only currently run 3 of the 26 required miles to complete a marathon – don't worry, your starting point doesn't matter… what matters is your results over time.

And, it may also occur to you that in order to be able to run 26 miles, it's not going to happen the next time you go running… or, even the subsequent 5 or 6 times you go running.

Therefore, you may be inclined to write down something like this:

Within 3 weeks, increase running capability from 3 miles per session to 6 miles per session.

Within 5 weeks, increase running capability from 3 miles per session to 10 miles per session.

Within 10 week, increase running capability from 3 miles per session to 17 miles per session.

And, so on…

Then, you could take it a step further and write down a schedule as to when you will run and how many miles you will run each time. And, when you stick to your plan without giving up, you'll find that it becomes easier and easier to accomplish the subsequent steps and reach your goal.

Naturally, your self-discipline will have increased and you'll have a much better awareness of who you are and what you can accomplish when you stick to your plan(s) of action.

Health & Well-Being & Exercise & Sleep

As with any aspect in life, your health and well-being play a huge role.

Being well-rested and maintaining a well-balanced diet – as well as participating in regular exercise – can help you to make more rational decisions, think more clearly, and perform at a higher level than when you are tired or lacking proper nutrition.

When we are over-tired from lack of proper sleep, our ability to resist temptation can decrease and we are likely more apt to impulse decisions.

The brain can work very much like a muscle in the body – well, a supercharged, multi-tasking, multi-functional one at that. And, just like every other muscle in the body, there is only a certain amount of energy that can be expended per day before it becomes tired, less efficient, and eventually, low functioning.

On top of that, it's been shown that we are not always able to accurately surmise just how tired / fatigued our body and brain may be.

Energy gets used up every day – we create more energy for ourselves with proper diet and sleep. But, even with the highest level of energy for our own body, at some point it will get drained and need to be renewed.

Therefore, proper rest and sleep are vital to maintaining high-performance brain function – which directly affects your self-discipline level.

The same holds true for proper nutrition. The better the dietary behavior, the more efficiently the body can convert food into an energy source. And, the more 'full' our internal energy source is, the better we can function physically and mentally throughout the course of a day.

There is a reciprocating relationship between regular exercise and self-discipline.

When you exercise, you increase blood flow throughout your body, including to your brain. You also release chemicals in the brain (endorphins) when you exert yourself to a certain point.

As the blood flows to the brain, more nutrients are brought to it and the brain is energized. When your brain is energized, it is strengthened and you're able to process thoughts more efficiently.

Self-discipline is at its strongest when your brain is functioning efficiently.

Conversely, the stronger your self-discipline, the more easy it becomes to exercise regularly – especially, for people who are not normally very motivated to exercise.

So, by strengthening your self-discipline, you're able to exercise more or for longer, which then strengthens the brain and thereby allows for a strengthened self-discipline.

Martial Arts, Yoga, Or Other Physical Discipline

While this book won't cover the scope of these physical disciplines, a physical, repeatable practice is an element that can significantly improve your self-discipline.

The practice of martial arts, such as Taekwondo, can significantly help your physical self-discipline. It also directly and indirectly helps increase your mental self-discipline through the practice of self-control.

You'll need to decide for yourself if a martial arts practice is appropriate for you, and which one may fit your goals and lifestyle. But, with so many available, you certainly have a multitude of ways to increase your self-discipline through physical activity.

Yoga, in all forms, is essentially self-discipline manifested into a physical realm.

Yoga teaches you to stretch, and fold, and contort, and (most importantly) control your body in a way that you likely won't do in normal circumstances. It teaches you physical control as well as mental control; and, it allows you to gain a greater understanding of who you are, how your body feels, and where your weaknesses may lie.

The mental aspect to yoga training has also been shown to be a proven stress reducer and a calming mechanism that allows you to increase your productivity and happiness. It's been shown to positively affect areas of the brain that help increase self-control and overall well-being.

Whichever physical activity you choose, maintaining your health and well-being is of the utmost importance – especially, when it comes to self-control. And, you'll find that the more you work on it, the better you'll become in many areas of life.

Relation To Personal Finance / Spending

Your money habits are usually a good indication of your overall self-discipline.

If you have a tendency to spend beyond your means, regularly find yourself short on money for what you want most / need, and constantly seem to accumulate meaningless 'stuff' while not improving your overall life and lifestyle, you likely need to improve your self-discipline.

If you are regularly in control of your spending, make rational and smart decisions with your money, are able to save for a emergencies, and never buy what you don't need, you've likely found a level of success in self-discipline.

It's a well-known fact that most lottery winners eventually end up spending all of their winnings and getting into debt within a few years after their triumph.

Many professional athletes, actors, musicians, and artists have also gone completely broke a few years after their prime and after they've signed a lucrative contract.

They've made poor financial choices and decisions, they've overspent their budget, they've not taken into account that the money may not always continue to flow in, and they've sometimes become 'caught up in the moment' when it comes to the glamour of success and fortune.

The essence of this is truly a lack of self-discipline.

Much of this has to do with the misconception that 'money = happiness'. This is simply not the case. Money is a tool that allows us to have and do more. But, having and doing more does not necessarily mean that you will be happier.

Therefore, it's always wise to setup a plan of money management – and, then be sure to stick to it. Whether it is budgeting, a savings plan, and investment plan, a purchase plan, or some combination of them, the most important part of the plan is to stick to it... unless you need to make minor adjustments and adaptations.

The longer you stick to the plan, the more you'll realize that money is simply an object that helps 'get' stuff, but doesn't serve a purpose for internal emotions... you likely won't be happy just sitting on a pile of money or counting it every day; you'll be happier with the way it allows you to do your favorite things, eat your favorite foods, and buy your favorite stuff.

And, as your money discipline gets stronger, you'll also find your overall self-discipline gets stronger. When you're less likely to impulsively spend your money because you believe it will make you happier (or, simply because you're compelled to do something with it), you'll find your impulses in other areas of life as also much more subdued. You'll make more rational decisions overall.

There are many methods for improving your money management self-discipline.

Some are as simple as making sure that you save x% of your money each pay period by putting it into a savings or money market account.

Other methods include adhering to a strict spending policy, such as $x per week is used for groceries, $x per week is used for other household expenses, $x per week is used for 'fun' or 'play' money, and $x per week is to be placed in a bank account for emergencies only.

More fun methods include the 'Jar Method' of managing your money – which provides a visual and touchable way to separate your money into sectionalized spending containers.

However you decide to plan your money management, the MOST IMPORTANT aspect is that you stick to it. If you diverge once, you'll be tempted to diverge repeatedly. If you take from your emergency savings to purchase a non-essential thing, you'll be tempted to do so again in the future. And, then you'll find that your emergency savings have disappeared – perhaps, even when you need them most.

As with any other area in life, self-control with money is not easy. And, the more money you have, the more temptations there are to spend it, share it, use it, abuse it, and eventually lose it.

It doesn't matter what financial level you're at right now… because, *right now* is the best time for you to start practicing better money management habits.

Accept Life For What It Is, Focus On What It Can Be

Let's face it… life is what it is. Some factors in life simply will not change, and others will change – sometimes, after a period of time.

A part of self-discipline is to recognize the factors in life that cannot be changed… and, to find a way to compensate / accommodate for them.

The more time you try to spend moving an immovable object, the less time you have to focus your attention and energy on moving forward.

Once you recognize what cannot be changed and have adjusted / adapted to that, you're then able to focus your attention on what *can* be changed.

One means of achieving a better perspective in life is to understand and accept that society, the world, and the universe aren't focused on your individual life – you simply aren't the center of everything.

In fact, other than your close-nit group of friends, family, and loved ones, the rest of the universe mostly doesn't care one tidly-squat of what happens to you in your life, whether positively or negatively.

So, you can't expect things to always go your way, you can't expect to have things handed to you, you can't expect things to always work out, and you can't expect that you'll always win.

Once you can come to terms with that, you'll soon discover that it's okay – that you're okay with some things being beyond your control… even in your own life.

And, when you learn which things are beyond your control, you'll be better able to focus your attention on the aspects of your life that are well within your control and can be modified, adjusted, tweaked, removed, added, or replaced.

Positive Thinking

Self-discipline and positive thinking work hand-in-hand, feeding off of each other symbiotically.

By thinking positively about the future and about your goals – for example, repeating the phrase "I can do this" – you'll generally find that your motivation and dedication to completing necessary steps has increased.

Subsequently, as you stick to your plan and complete your goals (and, potentially build your success), you'll likely find that your ability to think positively and confidently also increases.

Self-discipline and positive thinking work hand-in-hand, feeding off of each other symbiotically.

By thinking positively about the future and about your goals – for example, repeating the phrase "I can do this" – you'll generally find that your motivation and dedication to completing necessary steps has increased.

Subsequently, as you stick to your plan and complete your goals (and, potentially build your success), you'll likely find that your ability to think positively and confidently also increases.

Accepting / Tolerating Distress & Discomfort (Emotional & Physical)

One aspect to self-discipline is the ability to tolerate and / or accept emotional and physical discomfort.

This can be as simple as going a few steps further when we are tired or unmotivated during a run, walk, or jog. It can mean a few extra 'reps' when lifting weights, even though our muscles may be quite tired and / or sore.

This can also mean continuing to study or work on a project, even when one's eyes are tired or one really wants to go to bed or take a nap – within reason, of course, as we must always be mindful of our health and well-being.

In more extreme circumstances, it can mean accepting that sometimes what we want in life is not immediately available to us – and, enduring difficult times where we're unable to have what we want may require us to practice even more patience and self-discipline than we had anticipated.

An example of this would be during a significant relationship issue with someone you love and treasure.

There may come a time where the two of you encounter a relationship-changing disagreement or situation where one or both of you are greatly affected, hurt, and / or exasperated by what has happened.

And, it may be frustrating, painful, or emotionally-draining to the point where you're simply ready to give up and move on.

However, if you truly care about this person and if you're truly ready to continue your life with them, this is the deciding point where you can choose to stay dedicated through difficulty and hold on to your faith – even through the extreme discomfort or distress – or, you can simply call it quits.

Of course, not every relationship will work out... in life, there are times where one or both people in a relationship may change and be ready to move on.

But, in the case that you want it to work out, developing your self-discipline to endure the difficult challenges and navigate through the fear, pain, doubt, and misunderstanding is the only way to get to the other side successfully together.

Meditation And / Or Focused Breathing

There's a reason why meditation, which started many thousands of years ago, is still taught and practiced today – *it works.*

The scope of this book doesn't cover all of the practices of meditation or all of the benefits; however, there are many ways in which meditation can directly improve your self-discipline.

Meditation is a practice, much like lifting weights at a gym or running / cycling.

However, instead of working out and strengthening a physical muscle, you're strengthening your 'attention' through repetition and focus.

Mindfulness

Mindfulness is simply placing your attention or focus on the movement of your abdomen (belly) when you breath in and out and / or on the air passing in and out of your nostrils.

One way to easily accomplish this is to simply sit with your eyes closed and repeat the words 'inhale' and 'exhale' over and over as you breath in and out.

When applying this practice – 5 minutes a day, a few days a week – you begin to be able to slow your thoughts down, lower your anxiety, and resist impulses for immediate gratification.

Studies have actually proven this to be true. The University of Massachusetts Medical School – in association with The Harvard Medical School and Bender Institute of Neuroimaging – has stated that "mindfulness practice leads to increases in regional brain gray matter density."

They also stated that "mindfulness meditation has been reported to produce positive effects on psychological well-being that extend beyond the time the individual is formally meditating."

The University of Washington – in association with the University of Arizona – states that they "found that the meditation group… reported significantly greater mindful awareness and attention after meditation training."

They went on to say that their "study thus provides evidence that meditation training may be useful in the workplace, it also points to the benefits of relaxation."

In Practice

This book is not meant to be a guide on proper meditation techniques. There are experts around the world who can teach you methods of meditating and provide you with practices to improve your abilities.

However, there are three easy steps to simple meditation that you can take every day. And, every day you practice – like a muscle – you'll strengthen the part of your brain that is centered on concentration and self-discipline.

1) Sit Still For 5-45 minutes (your choice on the time frame)
2) Focus your attention on each inhale and exhale (you can even say "breath in" / "breath out" during the process
3) Any time you notice that your mind is wandering, bring the focus back to your breathing by saying "breath in" / "breath out again

These steps alone, when practiced daily, can help you improve your focus, your concentration, and your self-discipline by strengthening your mind through repetition.

Overcoming Temptation

Most self-discipline articles, blogs, and reports will tell you that one of the best things to do is to avoid temptation – to remove these factors from your life so that you are never distracted by them.

In an ideal world (or, in an unchanging vacuum), this would be a great practice.

However, at least with most people, real life contains constant distractions, temptations, and vices that create the opportunity for us to be led astray.

So, rather than the removal of these vices, a better practice is to learn how to overcome the internal temptation that arrives when these factors are present.

In some ways, this may include continuing to allow yourself to be exposed to temptation and vices so that you can build up a resistance against them. It may also include mentally coaching yourself to not desire or be tempted by these vices as much.

You can practice thoughts such as replacements: "I feel like I really want this… but, it is not good for me. Instead, if I have this other thing, I can have a similar pleasure or fulfillment without the negative effects."

You can also physically replace the temptation with a substitute – if your issue is with eating unhealthy foods, simply fill your cabinets and refrigerator with more healthy foods and remove the unhealthy ones.

If you're temptation every time you are inside your home is to lay on the couch or bed and watch TV, go outside of your couch or into another room.

These simple replacements, while perhaps not as satisfying as the original temptation, can help reduce your compulsion to engaging your vice.

Repetition & Practice

The only way to reinforce self-discipline so that it becomes second nature is through practice and repetition.

You need to focus on repeating the processes you develop for yourself when it comes to self-discipline.

Whether it's a physical routine, mental thought process, or meditation, repeating and continuing to repeat the process will help you become stronger (physically, emotionally, and / or spiritually) and help you increase your own self-discipline.

The Big Stuff First

One good practice to working on is to complete any difficult, challenging, large, or uncomfortable tasks or goals first.

As you now know, the brain has a limited supply of energy to be used each day before it needs a break. And, if you use up this energy on the smaller, lesser important tasks and duties, you'll have less 'oomph' left for the bigger, more important things.

Therefore, it's vital to start each of your days by prioritizing which tasks, duties, or activities will require the most attention and try to take them on first.

The more you work on this – like a muscle – the stronger and more comfortable you will be at doing this.

Routine is also very good for this process. As we make dozens (if not hundreds) of decisions per day, our energy is slowly used up with each subsequent choice.

When you create a repeatable routine, you start to eliminate more of the day-to-day decisions that you'd need to make (when to brush your teeth, what shirt to wear, what time to go to the gym, what time to study / do work, what time to take a shower / bath, and so on).

Your routine can be anything you want – but, as this routine becomes more and more familiar, you'll spend less time thinking about it… and, this will leave more brain energy for the decisions that require more of your attention.

Of course, you can't always take on the biggest things at once... but, focusing on what you can accomplish in terms of the most mentally-challenging first and then allowing yourself to ease into the less mentally-strenuous later in the day are a great way to ensure that you'll get through your goals.

Develop Healthy Habits

Ensure that you're always focused on what is best for you physically, emotionally, and psychologically. When you've found that routine or method, stick to it until it becomes habit.

The more you work on it, the easier it will become. And, the more second-nature it becomes, the less you energy you will have to expend on accomplishing it.

When action becomes habit, it becomes repeatable. So, make sure that the habits you develop are, in fact, healthy.

Reward / Incentivize Yourself

Life is short, and it sometimes leaves little time for enjoying ourselves – especially, when we are busy with work, family, and household activities.

Therefore, it's important to ensure that you're rewarding yourself for your accomplishments – especially, when your accomplishment comes after resisting certain negative or counter-productive temptations.

Any time you complete a goal and recognize the distractions and temptations that were put in front of you, yet you were able to ignore, avoid, or resist them, give yourself a pat on the back and treat yourself to something that is special to you (a particularly decadent food, a short vacation or trip, a new accessory, or any other 'thing' that you appreciate and enjoy).

It's important to recognize your own job-well-done, and to reinforce a confirmation that self-discipline is worth.

Much the same, you can set up incentives for reaching certain goals and / or resisting certain temptations.

If your goal is to lose weight, perhaps you can reward yourself with a small delectable treat for every day or every week that you do not break from our dietary plan or exercise regimen.

If your goal is complete a large project, school assignment, or work task within a certain period of time, give yourself small rewards for completing certain aspects within a preset time frame.

Again, these rewards can be anything you choose, but they are there to serve two purposes:

1. To motivate you to stick to the plan and / or accomplish your goal(s)
2. To acknowledge that you did a good job to this point and reinforce the habit of sticking to self-discipline.

Your Imagination As Substitute

This is one aspect of self-discipline that many people either do not really think about or do not participate in as a form of practice.

Sometimes, we desire things that simply cannot be gained or achieved... at least, not at the present moment.

In these circumstances, having an active imagination and / or being able to daydream can certainly help ease the frustration of not having what we want.

In addition, filling our mind with positive thoughts and day dreams can distract us from the temptations that lie in front of us.

One method that also helps is to simply write down the desired outcome or quest. Write down in detail what it is that you want -- even if you think or know it's unachievable. Write down thought by thought what you do, what you would say, how it would look and sound, and how you would feel.

While this may or may not help lead you to that goal (it could, in fact, be an impossible dream), it can still create a form of satisfaction to write it all down after expressing your imagination. And, you can always go back and read it again any time you want.

If it is an achievable dream – even if very difficult – this step alone can be the difference between the extra added motivation and stimulation to get there or not.

The mind is a powerful tool; and, it's able to create ideas that may not have otherwise existed. It's also a powerful tool towards creating our own realities.

And, the more you use it, strengthen it, mold it, and stretch it, the more expansive your reality may become.

Wrap-Up

As self-discipline encompasses so many important areas of life, it is a vital aspect to growth, development, success, and happiness.

The misconception that self-discipline means some sort of empirical self-torture by forgoing all pleasures in life in place of enjoyment is far from the truth that self-discipline simply means a maintained focus on your goal(s), mission(s), desire(s), and belief(s).

Self-discipline takes dedication. It takes confidence and self-respect. It takes practice. It takes patience. And, it take courage.

It is not always easy to develop self-control – whether in terms of personal health (weight and exercise), mental health (positive thinking), education (studying), work or employment success (diligence and focusing on completing the most important tasks), or achievement. So, it requires you to continue to work on it, even through the rest of your life.

Sometimes, developing self-discipline can be intense, intimidating, or even downright frightening. So, being willing to show courage through the difficult challenges is the only way to get over the most foreboding obstacles.

You'll generally find that as you show more courage and take further steps towards your development, that things become easier and less intimidating.

And, from that point, less courage and more dedication is needed to continue.

You need to stay committed to your goals and your plan of action. If you create a method, a routine, or a list of steps to accomplish your goal(s), stick to it. Don't allow yourself to stray too far off of the path – you'll find that each time you stray, it becomes just a bit more difficult to resist the temptation to stray again.

When things get challenging, don't give up. Many times, implementing our plans of action is most difficult at the very beginning and at the very end. In fact, if you're finding the last steps very difficult to stick to, you actually could be so close to your goal that you could reach out to it.

This is the point where you just need to stay focused – stay committed to what you're looking to achieve.

If you're still finding it difficult, try repeating a simple phrase to yourself to maintain your motivation:

"I can do this"

"This is achievable"

"I'm almost there"

"I can't wait until I finish"

"I've come this far, it's only a little bit further"

And, any other number of phrases and mantras can help you get through the most difficult challenges.

Remember to positively reinforce both your accomplishments and your dedication to your goal. You deserve to reward yourself as you progress through your achievements.

Respect yourself. Give yourself ample time to accomplish your goals and don't punish yourself when you fall short.

Get to know who you really are and what you really want in life. When you have defined goals in front of you, it's easier to focus on accomplishing them.

Write down any goals (short- and long-term) that you may have so that you can review them when you feel like you're slipping.

Remember to take care of your body and mind through proper rest / sleep, exercise, and nutrition. The stronger your brain is, the easier it is to increase (and, use) your self-discipline and willpower.

And, never give up – even when things are most bleak and difficult.

www.ingramcontent.com/pod-product-compliance
Lightning Source LLC
Chambersburg PA
CBHW070342190526
45169CB00005B/2004